I0475965

Table of Contents

Executive Summary

Our rural communities are home to some of the most hard working and fiercely self-reliant Americans in the United States. Strong and secure rural communities are essential to creating an economy built to last that rewards hard work and responsibility—not outsourcing, loopholes, and risky financial deals. While the security of the middle class has been threatened by the irresponsible financial collapse and the worst economic downturn since the Great Depression, rural Americans continue to come together to work hard and make ends meet. The values that have helped hard-working, responsible families weather the storm continue to move our economy forward.

A agricultural economy built to last is integral to the affordability of our food, the independence of our energy supply, and the security of America's middle class. While there is still work to do, over the last few years, the U.S. agricultural economy has yielded encouraging results:

- Farm sector income experienced a rapid rebound since 2009, growing 27% in 2010 and 20% in 2011, according to preliminary estimates.

- Farm sector income reached a preliminary estimate of a nominal record of $98.1 billion in 2011. Adjusting for general inflation, real farm income in 2011 recorded its 3rd highest level in the last 50 years.

- Farm exports are at record levels: in FY 2011, total food and agriculture exports reached the highest level ever at $137.4 billion.

- In FY 2011, agricultural exports supported more than 1.15 million American jobs.

- The direct and indirect economic activity brought by farm exports supported 907,000 jobs in 2010, including 298,000 in the farm sector, 174,000 in manufacturing, and 437,000 in transportation and other service sectors.

- America's agricultural trade surplus is at a record level: in FY 2011, the surplus exceeded $42 billion.

The Administration has developed and implemented a comprehensive rural strategy to spur innovation, increase export levels, invest in clean energy, and expand opportunities for rural enterprises on and off the farm that create jobs.

These are part of broader efforts by the Administration to advance the economic security of Americans living in rural areas by, for example, improving educational opportunities, providing access to affordable healthcare, and investing in infrastructure. Last year, the President established the first-ever White House Rural Council which has been coordinating these efforts, working to streamline and improve the effectiveness of Federal programs serving rural America, and building on the progress detailed in last year's White House report Jobs and Economic Security for Rural America.

This report focuses specifically on the current state of the agricultural economy and the Administration's strategy to ensure an agricultural economy built to last. While the U.S. economy continues to recover from its worst recession since the 1930's and there is still more work to be done, America's agricultural economy—farms and other related businesses—has recovered more quickly than many other sectors. The total value added to the U.S. economy from the farm sector rose about 35% between the second quarter of 2009 and the fourth quarter of 2011. Rising global demand and increasing American productivity have made this turnaround possible. This report highlights the positive trends occurring in the agricultural economy and the efforts of the Administration to support those trends.

A strong agricultural economy is critical to a strong rural economy.

Strength in agricultural production supports other parts of the economy, particularly in rural communities. Farms and ranches buy fertilizer and seed, invest in farm machinery, contract out with custom operators, and support the many local businesses that come together to serve farms and farming families, including restaurants and health care service providers. High levels of production also benefit other businesses like grain elevators, biofuel refineries, and processed food manufacturers. According to the industry input-output accounts for 2010, every additional dollar of final output in the agriculture, forestry, fishing, and hunting industry raises gross output across all industries by approximately $2.20.

Under the Obama Administration, shipments of sectors upstream and downstream from agriculture, such as farm machinery and finished food products, have increased substantially. The following wide-reaching impacts of a strong agricultural economy underscore its fundamental importance to the U.S. economy:

- Farm machinery shipments reached nearly $3 billion in 2011, a record high; and

- Manufactured food product shipments exceeded $710 billion in 2011, a record high.

There are several factors driving progress in the American farm economy.

Innovation

In 1950, the average dairy cow produced about 5,300 pounds of milk—today the average cow produces about 22,000 pounds of milk due to improvements in cow genetics, feed formula, and management practices. Over that time period, the number of dairy cows in America has fallen by more than half, yet U.S. production has nearly doubled.

Studies find that every dollar invested in public agricultural research generates ten to twenty times that amount in benefits to society. Innovation in U.S. agriculture has kept America's farms among the most productive in the world. U.S. farm sector income reached a preliminary estimate of a nominal record of $98.1 billion in 2011. Adjusting for general inflation, real farm income in 2011 was recorded at its 3rd highest level in the last 50 years. Yet, there is still more work to do. The Administration plans to capitalize on the diverse opportunities and invest in future innovations, such as more productive crops, healthier livestock, and adaptive farming practices for weather extremes by requesting $2.3 billion in our 2013 Budget for agricultural research and development (R&D).

Increasing Agricultural Exports

While much work remains, successful efforts by the Federal government to open foreign markets have contributed to an agricultural export boom. During FY 2011, the Obama Administration resolved numerous unwarranted barriers to U.S. food and agricultural exports expanding and preserving agricultural trade valued at $4.1 billion. In FY 2011, American agricultural exports reached an all-time high of $137.4 billion, or roughly 11% of total exports for the fiscal year. Additionally, America runs a trade surplus in agricultural goods—a surplus that reached a record level of over $42 billion in FY 2011. The direct and indirect economic activity brought by farm exports supported 907,000 American jobs in 2010, including 298,000 in the farm sector, 174,000 in manufacturing, and 437,000 in transportation and other service sectors.

Fifty-seven countries have lifted import bans related to avian influenza on U.S. poultry products. Negotiations with eight other countries under the Trans-Pacific Partnership offer significant new export opportunities for U.S. farmers and ranchers and provide a foundation for expanding open markets to other Pacific Rim countries. Negotiating a new Memorandum of Understanding on beef has provided new access to American ranchers with an additional $140 million annually in beef exports to the European Union in 2011. The Obama Administration has negotiated two organic food equivalency arrangements with Canada and the European Union, which are expected to enhance trade in organic certified food products.

Once fully implemented, free trade agreements passed under this Administration with Korea, Panama, and Colombia are projected to boost U.S. agricultural exports by $2.3 billion per year. Opening South Korea's market to U.S. beef during negotiations for the Korea-U.S. free trade agreement more than doubled the value of U.S. beef exports to Korea from $294 million to $686 million between the years 2008 and 2011. The Administration is now negotiating a new trade agreement—the Trans Pacific Partnership—which will provide new market opportunities for America's farmers and ranchers. The Administration also continues to fight for America's farmers and ranchers to open export markets where they face unwarranted barriers.

Building a Clean Energy Economy

The President's all-of-the-above approach to harnessing every domestic energy source, including alternatives like biofuels, bioenergy, and wind power provide increasing opportunities for farmers, ranchers, and forest managers to contribute to U.S. energy security and greenhouse gas mitigation goals. The U.S. became a net exporter of ethanol in 2011 is on pace to produce more than 14 billion gallons of corn ethanol in 2012, accounting for about 40% of total U.S. corn use. Researchers have linked the increasing supply of ethanol between 2000 and 2010 to a drop in gasoline prices of approximately $0.25 per gallon on average. In addition, the U.S. produced 861 million gallons of biodiesel in 2011. Lastly, installed wind energy generation capacity has increased over the past three years from about 25,000 MW at the end of 2008 to almost 47,000 MW by the end of 2011. The pain at the pump, however, is still all too real. This Administration has led the effort to promote the domestic production and use of advanced biofuels with the potential to create hundreds of thousands of jobs in rural communities; by investing in research, supporting farmers growing bioenergy feedstocks, and helping to support more than 230 bioenergy projects, including construction of 5 commercial-scale biorefineries to produce fuels. Approximately 25,000 rural small businesses, farmers, and ranchers, save energy and improve their bottom line by installing renewable energy systems and energy efficiency solutions that will save a projected 6.5 billion in kWh—enough energy to power over 590,000 homes for a year.

While significant progress has been made, there is still more we can do. As part of his "To-Do List," the President has called on Congress to pass the production tax credit, which will play an essential role in supporting American businesses and American jobs in communities across the county, while also investing in American innovation. The Administration's commitment to an "all-of-the-above" energy strategy is starting to yield significant results for hard-working farmers, American energy independence, and the environment.

Promoting New Diverse Industries

The rich heritage of the agricultural economy features a range of new, diverse industries and sectors. Organic certifications, specialty crops, biobased products (products, such as fuels, chemicals, and power, that are developed from biological sources), and agri-tourism (agriculture-based tourism) are a few of the many domestic industries further diversifying the agricultural economy. The retail value of the organic industry grew to $31.4 billion in 2011, up from $21.1 billion in 2008. The number of operations certified organic grew by 1,109—or more than 6%—between 2009 and 2011. Specialty crops, such as fruit and tree nuts, generate approximately $18 billion in U.S. farm cash receipts, on average each year. Future growth of the agricultural economy can be enhanced by those alternative sectors.

Supporting Rural Communities

During the recession, rural communities pulled together to support one another. President Obama knows we must continue to support those who work hard and play by the rules. The growth of the agricultural economy has had carryover effects on the rural economy at large and can be directly linked to the policies and priorities advanced by President Obama. But there's still work to be done. The values that helped so many push through the worst economic downturn since the Great Depression must continue to help families carve a path to the middle class. President Obama understands that the strength of the rural economy depends on its hard-working communities. That's why the Obama Administration has invested in over 6,250 new rural community facilities projects, over 12,000 grants and loans to assist over 50,000 rural small businesses. These investments reward hard work and responsibility and help rural businesses expand, grow and innovate. They also help us look after our own by increasing access to telemedicine opportunities for 1,440 schools and 3,925 medical facilities, improving the availability of quality health care and education in rural America.

Overall, the U.S. agricultural economy stands on the cusp of a historic opportunity for export-led growth. It will require continued investments in rural economies, new science and technology, alternative energy sources, and effective international trade policies. The Administration's work to date on these issues shows that President Obama is committed, now more than ever, to the values and standards that will help hard-working communities realize this potential.

U.S. Agriculture and Rural America

The agricultural economy is more resilient today than it was thirty years ago during the farm crisis that spilled over into rural America. At that time, interest rates hikes driven by the Federal Reserve and other Western central banks led to a sharp slowdown in economic activity domestically and abroad. As rising debt-service burdens and plummeting exports squeezed economies, developing countries' demand for U.S. agricultural products collapsed. American farmers had borrowed large sums in the hopes of selling into an ever-growing international market, and then found their own debt payments escalating as their revenues declined. Farm foreclosures soared, and farmers sharply reduced their investment expenditures on new farm equipment. The value of U.S. agricultural exports fell by a third between 1980 and 1986. Real farm sector asset values fell by nearly half in that period. A full recovery from that crisis took nearly two decades.

During those lean years, the less efficient farms—the ones with higher costs and lower output per unit of input—simply could not survive. The most productive farms became a larger and larger part of the total industry, while the least productive farms disappeared. This made the industry as a whole much more productive. It was a difficult process, but at its end America had a more efficient, more resilient agricultural system. Investments in rural America benefited farm families and helped boost production. Farmers diversified income streams and hedged against risks by renting lands, specializing in management of farming operations, contracting capital-intensive services requiring expensive machinery and information services, and making greater use of output contracts and financial risk mitigation strategies. Moreover, production has shifted to farm corporations and partnerships. Those factors have spread risk across a wider set of stakeholders. Farms have become more efficient and productive, increasing output without increasing inputs.

The resulting resilience and increased productivity has helped the agricultural economy rebound quickly from the recent recession. Since the farm crisis of the mid-1980s, real farm assets (including land and buildings) have risen in both nominal and real (inflation-adjusted) terms (see Figure 1). In real terms, farm assets had not reached their 1980 level until this year. Similarly, agricultural land values are now at record highs today.

Today, the real equity of farms is expected to establish a new nominal record in 2012, with the real value of farm assets at the highest level since 1980. In 2007, 31% of farms used debt financing, as compared to 60% in 1986 (Henderson and Akers, 2010). Current levels of

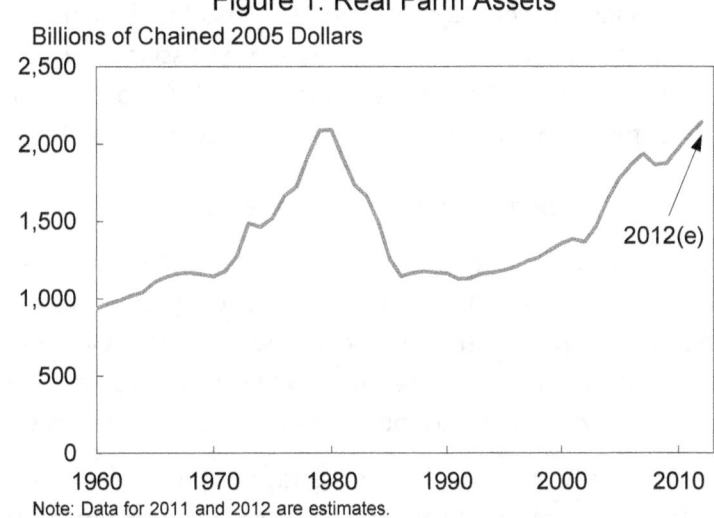

Figure 1: Real Farm Assets
Billions of Chained 2005 Dollars

Note: Data for 2011 and 2012 are estimates.
Source: USDA Economic Research Service.

debt are well below debt repayment capacity, with larger farms making more use of their debt capacity (Sundell and Shane, 2012).

Strong demand creates higher commodity prices and higher output levels. As a result, the total value added to the U.S. economy from the farm sector, which represents the sum of income earned by all of the factors of agriculture production, rose about 32% on net between the second quarter of 2009, the quarter identified by the National Bureau of Economic Research as the business cycle trough, and the first quarter of 2012 (see red line in Figure 2). Nominal income growth from the agriculture sector during the recovery outpaced growth from the nonfarm business sector.

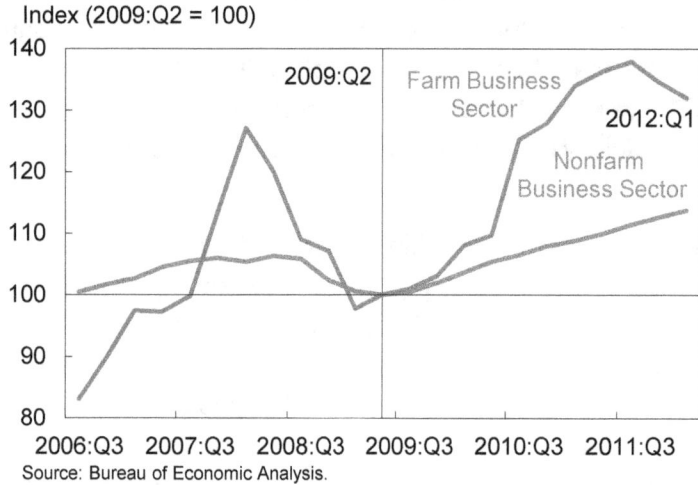

Figure 2: Value Added in the Farm and Nonfarm Business Sectors

Index (2009:Q2 = 100)

Source: Bureau of Economic Analysis.

Spillovers from our strong agricultural sector boost domestic sales, trade, and GDP. As a result of strong agricultural productivity growth, the U.S. has been able to devote the equivalent of 25 percent of acreage to production for export. Increasing incomes abroad, a depreciating dollar, and a continuing comparative advantage in agriculture from productivity growth have produced U.S. agricultural trade surpluses. Farm exports, besides being a source of U.S. economic growth, are one of the bright spots in the economic recovery. Growing global demand and increasing American productivity have helped the U.S. agricultural sector take advantage of new market opportunities. The growing middle class in China, for example, has resulted in U.S. corn and soybean exports to China surging to record levels over the past two years. As discussed later in this report the Obama Administration has won major gains for U.S. agricultural exporters by removing substantial non-science based barriers to our agricultural exports and by passing and implementing three new free trade agreements. With three new free trade agreements with Korea, Colombia and Panama entering into effect in 2012, U.S. food and agricultural exports are expected to continue to be strong.

Agricultural Economy Benefits Rural America

America's agricultural revival coupled with smart public investments is providing a vital source of new economic opportunity for rural America. The agricultural sector is tightly linked to the larger nonfarm economy as the purchaser of production inputs—such as fertilizer and farm machinery—and the provider of agricultural commodities for direct human and animal consumption or for use in downstream industries—such as finished food products or biofuels refineries.

Those linkages between rural America and agricultural producers are often national or global in nature. Manufacturing farm production inputs (such as machinery and fertilizers) benefit from strong farm incomes and increasing demand for expanded production. Also, farm services and food processing, which are disproportionately located in non-metropolitan counties, have also rebounded quickly (up 17%) since 2009 and are near historic levels.

Box 1: Farm machinery sales have been expanding.

Buoyed by higher incomes for farmers and expanding demand for U.S. agricultural products, U.S. shipments from farm machinery companies rebounded quickly from the recent economic downturn (see Figure 3), reaching a record high of more than $29 billion in 2011. 2012 looks to be another bumper year. The Federal Reserve Bank of Kansas City reports that "loans for farm machinery and equipment held at high levels with a sharp jump in the volume of intermediate-term loans" (Henderson and Akers, 2012). Prospects are good, even for dealers who specialize in sending second-hand tractors abroad (*National Public Radio*, March 13, 2012, "Record-High Food Prices Boost Farmers' Bottom Lines"). Several large farm machinery companies in the U.S. are gearing up for expanded opportunities at home and abroad. Deere & Co. (headquartered in Moline, IL), for example, project a 10% increase in farm machinery sales in the U.S. and Canada this year (see *Financial Times* May 16, 2012) and point to rising global populations coupled with rapid per capita GDP growth, especially in large emerging markets like India and China, as sources of continued growth in product demand. Those domestic and international prospects translate into domestic manufacturing jobs. In December 2011, Deere & Co. announced plans to invest $85 million in its Ankeny, Iowa plant, to upgrade and expand production capacity for self-propelled sprayers. The investments are expected to preserve or create 400 jobs at that plant. More recently, Deere & Co. reported investing $70 million to expand production of large farm tractors at the Waterloo, Iowa plant. The plant currently ships tractors to more than 130 countries each year and employs roughly 6,000 workers. Another prominent farm machinery manufacturer AGCO (headquartered in Duluth, Georgia) recently renovated and expanded its Massey Ferguson tractor production facility in Jackson, Minnesota (population 3,300), at a cost of $6.2 million.

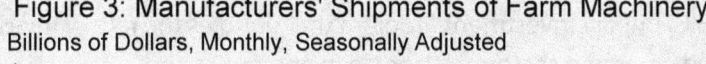

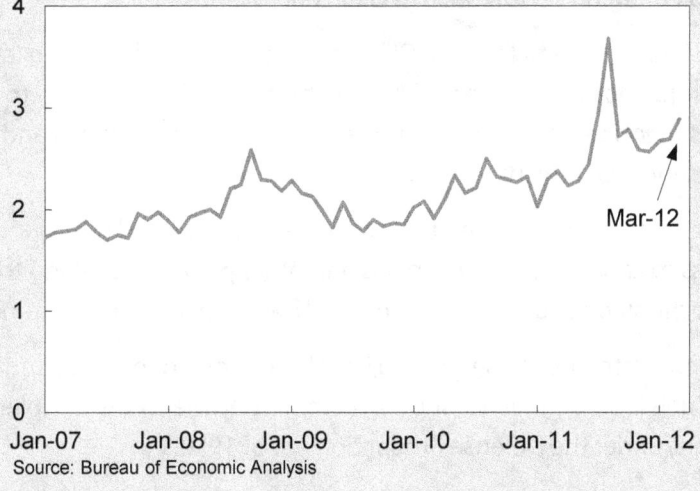

Figure 3: Manufacturers' Shipments of Farm Machinery
Billions of Dollars, Monthly, Seasonally Adjusted

Source: Bureau of Economic Analysis

The family farmer has always been a cornerstone of America. The Obama Administration is committed to supporting and incentivizing beginning family farmers in order to support their efforts in providing healthy, American-grown food for our country. In addition, the Administration is dedicated to helping already existing family famers stay prosperous and stay on their land. In 1945 the average age of the American farmer was 39; today it is 60. That means now more than ever the policies that the President is putting in place to support new and existing family farmers are essential to sustaining our nation's food supply. In order to accomplish this, the Obama Administration has provided more than $5 billion in farm operating and ownership loans to help over 35,000 small and medium sized businesses. There are policies being created to ensure new farmers are given the tools and competitive edge to succeed in a competitive market.

However, despite a strong agricultural economy, rural America faces a number of unique challenges. First, incomes are lower and poverty rates are higher in rural areas than they are in urban areas. Second, a lower proportion of the rural population is of working age (20-64), and the share of the U.S. population living in rural counties has steadily declined over time. Third, a higher portion of rural residents are on disability and therefore unable to participate in the rural workforce. Fourth, educational attainment lags behind that of urban areas for the working-age population.

Recognizing these challenges, this Administration reaffirmed its commitment to investing in rural America. On June 9, 2011, President Obama issued Executive Order 13575, which established the White House Rural Council. At its core, the Rural Council has taken steps to: (1) increase capital flow to rural areas and improve job creation and workforce development; (2) enhance telecommunications in rural areas, support renewable energy efforts, and open new markets for rural communities; (3) expand access to health care services, improve education, and housing; and (4) promote outdoor recreational opportunities to generate economic growth.

Some key examples of the Rural Council's successes include:[1]

- The Administration established a rural component within the Small Business Investment Company (SBIC) Impact Investment Program that doubles the rate of investment in distressed rural areas and emerging sectors such as clean energy.

- USDA and the Department of Labor (DOL) partnered to offer job training information and better utilize the rural footprint of the USDA field offices across the country to provide them with greater access to job search resources by reducing the driving times and distances for rural customers seeking program information.

- USDA and the Department of Health and Human Services (HHS) signed an agreement to improve access to capital for rural hospitals and other providers seeking to implement health information technology and expand the health IT workforce in rural communities.

- The Navy, the Department of Energy, and USDA have joined forces to spur the creation of an advanced biofuels industry that will support commercial aviation, with a pledge of $510 million, over three years, under the Defense Production Act of 1950.

- Through the White House Rural Council's efforts, the Administration has directed Federal agencies to take additional steps to double the purchase of biobased products over the next two years, creating new rural jobs and driving innovation where biobased products are grown

---

1. For more Rural Council initiative details, see: www.WhiteHouse.gov/administration/eop/rural-council

and manufactured. Additionally, the Administration will increase by 50% the number of new products that are designated as biobased by February 2013.

- In January 2012, President Obama signed an Executive Order creating a Task Force charged with developing a National Travel and Tourism Strategy with recommendations for new policies and initiatives to promote travel opportunities throughout the United States, including tourism opportunities in rural communities. The Task Force has completed the National Travel and Tourism Strategy, and agencies have already begun undertaking actions (alone and in partnership with the private sector) to drive additional tourism this summer and fall.

- USDA and the Department of the Interior (DOI) established the Working Lands for Wildlife partnership to work with farmers, ranchers, and forest landowners and use innovative approaches to restore and enhance the habitats focusing of seven at-risk wildlife species. In return for voluntarily making habitat improvements on their lands, the Federal government will provide landowners with regulatory certainty that they will not be asked to take additional conservation actions.

- USDA's Forest Service, in conjunction with the White House Rural Council, released a strategy to increase the scale of restoration treatments like forest thinning, reforestation, and other activities to restore and sustain the health of our forests.

- The Administration announced an initiative to assist rural homeowners refinance their mortgages at lower interest rates through USDA's Rural Development agency. By reallocating existing funding, at no additional cost to taxpayers, USDA will have almost doubled the amount of funds available to homeowners seeking to lower their mortgage payments or avoid foreclosure.

- About 65% of all interstate highway miles—and 70% of all Federal-aid highway miles—run through rural areas.[2] These highways allow rural Americans to sell their products in key markets throughout the country and the world. Beyond highways, Federal programs also support the rail, barge, and ocean-going transportation infrastructures. Without this key infrastructure, the crops grown in rural America could not as easily reach the domestic and international markets that sustain farm income.

- Through efforts such as the USDA's Farm to School Program and its Know Your Farmer, Know Your Food initiative, the Administration is working to better connect consumers and farmers and to encourage consumers to learn more about the people behind the products and the role of agriculture in our economy and communities. These efforts are yielding results. As of mid-2011, there were over 7,175 farmers markets operating throughout the United States. This is a 17 percent increase from 2010. Nearly 110,000 farms across the nation are linked to farmers markets. On average, those farms reported that local food sales accounted for 61 percent of their total sales. Almost two-thirds of these producers, regardless of size, reported that local food sales were at least seventy-five percent of their total sales.

---

2. CEA report (2010)

Promoting Agricultural Research and Technological Innovation

Persistent gains in efficiency have defined American agriculture. Over time, aided and abetted by public and private investments in agricultural R&D, U.S. farmers have consistently found ways to grow more with less. Whereas growth in U.S. industrial output over the past 50 years has mostly been due to increases in non-labor and labor inputs; agricultural output growth has mainly been due to substantial increases in total factor productivity (TFP) (see Figure 4).

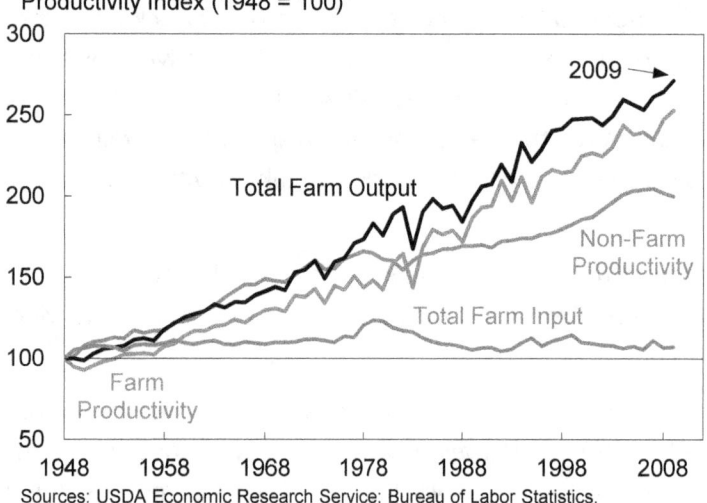

Figure 4: Farm and Non-Farm Productivity
Productivity Index (1948 = 100)

Sources: USDA Economic Research Service; Bureau of Labor Statistics.

American farmers have continually found a way to grow more with less: new seeds are less susceptible to disease and yield more crops; new tractors are guided by satellites and spread fertilizer optimally across the field; and animals' diets are optimally calibrated to grow larger animals with less feed. For example, corn yields remained relatively constant from the Civil War through WWII; but yield jumped from 33 bushels per acre in 1945 to 100 bushels per acre in 1979 to an estimated 166 bushels per acre today. The same is true for animals.

There were less than half as many dairy cows in the U.S. in 2010 as in 1950, but milk production per cow was about four times as high, due to improvements in cow genetics, feed formulations, and management practices. In poultry, broiler chickens today consume about 1.8 pounds of feed to generate one pound of weight gain, as compared to 2.1 pounds in 1980 and 2.9 pounds in 1955. Improvements in feed conversion reduce feed costs for livestock producers, and they also reduce the amount of manure generated per pound of meat produced or feed used.

Innovations from Investments in Research and Development (R&D)

Increasing productivity on U.S. farms stems largely from the rapid and widespread adoption of an ongoing series of biological, chemical, mechanical, and organizational advances. Formal research programs are carried out in universities, government labs, and private firms. Similarly, most agricultural innovations building off that research are developed by input suppliers in the private sector or by public institutions.

Agricultural research and development generates high payoffs for farmers and the public. Heisey et al. (2010) notes that the substantial body of literature on investing in agricultural R&D shows that the social benefits from public research in agriculture have been large, with social rates of return usually falling within the range of 20 to 60 percent annually (see also Fuglie and Heisey, 2007, for a recent overview, and Alston et al. (2010) or Evenson (2001) for extensive surveys).

Expenditures on public and private R&D programs provide much of the impetus for new technological innovations (see Figure 5). Total public and private R&D spending in agriculture reached $11 billion dollars in 2007, or nearly 8% of the value-added in the sector. Annual public R&D spending, through universities as well as government laboratories, rose by 77% between 1970 and 2002 (after accounting for inflation), and played an important role in driving productivity. Private R&D expenditures doubled (after accounting for inflation) between 1970 and 2007 (see Figure 5).

Innovation leads to Increasingly Efficient Farms

Efficiency-increasing agricultural innovations have enabled farmers to manage more cropland or raise more livestock. In addition, innovations have led farms to contract out for specialized services.

Farmers now rely extensively on private consultants, government extension agents, lenders, and supplier representatives for technical advice.

Some of these managerial innovations rely on further developments in the design of organizations and of contractual relationships in order to effectively organize a series of complicated commercial relationships. The share of production under marketing or production contracts increased from 28% in 1993 to over 38% by 2010. Corn, soybean, and wheat producers, for

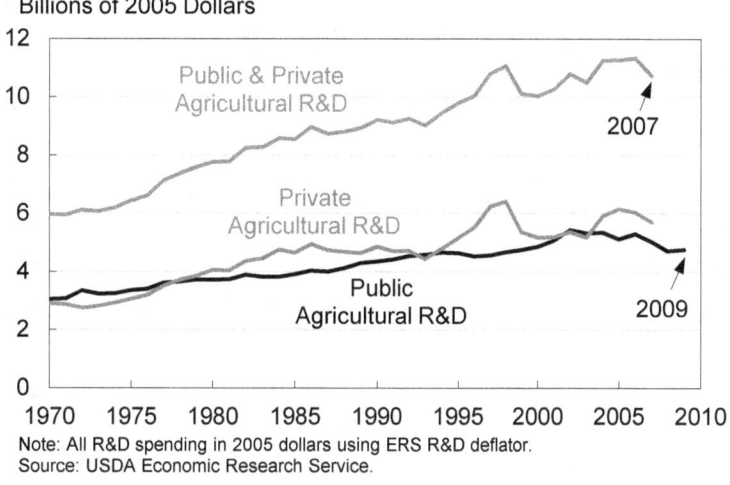

Figure 5: Public and Private U.S. Agricultural R&D Spending, 1971-2009

Billions of 2005 Dollars

Note: All R&D spending in 2005 dollars using ERS R&D deflator.
Source: USDA Economic Research Service.

example, place about half of their production under forward contracts; many of them also invest in storage facilities to store products when anticipating future price increases, and nearly 30% of them use futures markets to hedge the risks from their cash sales (MacDonald and Korb, 2011). Similarly, farmers have realized more intensive use of capital by leasing equipment from specialized suppliers, and they often engage further specialized expertise, and capital equipment, by contracting for certain farm tasks (such as spraying, field preparation, or harvesting) with custom service providers.

Farmers now use information technology to automatically vary feed mixes and climate controls to the precise needs of the animals in confined feeding operations. Dairy farmers can monitor feed intake, milk production, and milk attributes on a near-continuous basis to identify animal health threats and the effectiveness of feed formulations. Integrated hog operations, for example, sharply reduced the amount of feed, capital and labor needed to produce hogs as new technologies and organizational forms swept the industry. As a result, live hog prices were nearly a third lower than they would have been without the productivity growth that occurred between 1992 and 2004, and retail pork prices were 9% lower (Key and McBride, 2007).

The market, scientific, and technological opportunities beckoning American farmers are as great as they have ever been. Our focus therefore is on practical application of science, research and development on America's farms and ranches. Even America's larger firms are too small to support sophisticated basic research, and many of the most significant applications of farm improvement research are not patentable. Public science institutions and the private farm partnerships must continue to realize the possibilities within the Agricultural economy. The Obama Administration believes America's agricultural future is worth investing in, and has committed to increases in scientific research that could benefit our agricultural sector for decades to come.

America's Agricultural Export Boom Powers an Agricultural Revival

The collapse of farm export markets in the 1980s triggered a crisis in America's agricultural economy whose effects were felt in rural communities for nearly two decades. In the 2000s, though, unexpectedly strong growth in a set of economies largely outside the set of traditional U.S. farm export destinations began to fundamentally reshape the contours of supply and demand for agricultural goods. Those countries included emerging markets whose economic progress had been uneven and halting since the 1970s. With strong growth throughout the developing world in the 2000s, those countries collectively represented an increasingly important source of demand for agricultural goods and other commodities.

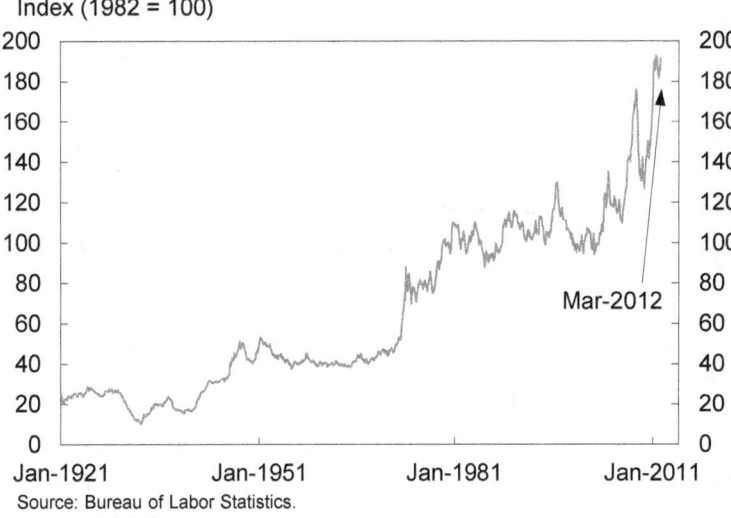

Figure 6: Farm Products Producer Price Index

Index (1982 = 100)

Source: Bureau of Labor Statistics.

Reflecting rising export demand, commodity prices began rising in the 2000s. Those price increases continued through the decade, reaching historically unprecedented levels by the eve of the global financial crisis.

Due to the world economic slowdown, between 2008 and 2009, U.S. agricultural exports fell from $115 billion to $98.5 billion. Total economic activity generated through farm exports fell from $273 billion in 2008 to $228 billion in 2009. Fortunately, this collapse was short-lived. As the world economy recovered, agricultural commodity prices rose (see Figure 6) and U.S. economic activity supported by farm exports soared to new heights.

The economic benefits brought by America's rapid farm export recovery are far greater than is generally understood. The nearly $116 billion of U.S. farm exports in 2010 generated an additional $155 billion in related domestic economic activity. The direct and indirect effects together accounted for a total $271 billion of U.S. national income. That larger number reflects the additional economic activity and employment opportunities that exist in concert with the agriculture sector. For example, products such as bulk grains require a large transportation system as they are moved from the farm to an elevator, to train cars or barges, and then to the port. In addition to the transportation system, high-value agricultural products create jobs in the processing and/or manufacturing sectors. All this direct and indirect economic activity generated by farm exports supported 907,000 jobs in 2010.[3] In FY 2011, total food and agricultural exports reached a record level of $137.4 billion.

These record-breaking achievements are a testament to the skill, hard work, and productivity of America's farmers and ranchers. They also point to the skill with which America's agricultural exporters have tapped into the growing demand generated by fast-growing emerging markets. Box 2 explains how rapid growth in these economies is creating the potential for even more dynamic growth and prosperity for our agricultural exporters in the years ahead. To fully benefit from this historic opportunity, though, America's farmers and ranchers need access to these growing markets, and a level playing field on which to compete. America's agricultural industry cannot negotiate these terms on its own—it needs the full support and engagement of the federal government's trade agencies.

Opening Global Markets to U.S. Agricultural Exports under the National Export Initiative

Even today, after a half century of multilateral trade negotiations, international trade in agricultural products remains distorted by high tariffs and unwarranted nontariff barriers. All too often, American exporters, seeking to feed a growing world, find restrictive trade policies standing between them and the foreign customers who could benefit from their products. These restrictive policies can be especially damaging to our agricultural exporters when they block access to the world's fastest growing markets. That is why emerging markets have been a particular focus of Obama Administration efforts to negotiate better agricultural market access. This Administration has signed historic free trade agreements to improve America's access to emerging markets, it has launched a new effort to negotiate free trade agreements in a region of the world economy that contains some of world's most dynamic emerging markets, and has fought unfair and unwarranted barriers to U.S. exports in emerging markets around the world.

Under the President's National Export Initiative (NEI), the Obama Administration has made reducing trade barriers to improve market access overseas for U.S. farmers and ranchers a top priority, alongside efforts to ensure that America's trading partners fully honor all the commitments they have made under existing trade agreements. Often trade barriers hide behind concerns for public safety and public health. For example, global concerns about avian influenza and H1N1 were invoked as an excuse for U.S. trading partners to implement widespread bans on U.S. exports of poultry and pork products. Use of phytosanitary standards that lack a clear basis in science continue to block U.S. agricultural exports to developing countries as well as some advanced industries economies. The European Union (EU), for example, is the fifth largest export market for U.S. agricultural products, but a range of U.S. products are kept out of the EU market because of EU or member state food safety rules and other barriers that are not scientifically justified. Currently, the United States and the EU are exploring possibilities for expanding transatlantic trade and investment. A priority for the Obama Administration in any new trade initiative with the EU will be to address unwarranted barriers to U.S. agricultural exports.

---

3. www.ers.usda.gov/Data/TradeMultiplier/econeffects/2010overview.aspx

To achieve the goals of the NEI, the President has signed several historic trade agreements that significantly expand market access for our agricultural exporters. The recently implemented U.S.-Korea Free Trade Agreement (KORUS) is set to deliver substantial gains for U.S. agricultural exports in coming years. In a separate beef import protocol concluded in 2008, Korea agreed to adjust its import restrictions on U.S. beef. As a result, U.S. beef exports to Korea more than doubled in value, 2008-2011, to about $686 million. Under KORUS, Korea will gradually bring its tariffs on imports of U.S. beef and pork down to zero and the U.S. meat industry will benefit from even greater gains in trade. The improved access provided by the agreement for a wide range of other products, beginning in 2012 and continuing over the agreement's phase-in period, will yield new market opportunities for U.S. exporters. USDA estimates that, when fully implemented, KORUS will expand U.S. agricultural exports to Korea by an estimated $1.9 billion per year—gains that will benefit agricultural producers and processors across the United States. Together with the free trade agreements with Panama and Colombia, passed at the same time, the three agreements, once implemented, are expected to boost U.S. agricultural exports by $2.3 billion per year (Wainio, Gehlhar, and Dyck, 2011).

The Obama Administration has worked with a number of other developing and developed countries to reopen their markets to U.S. beef products. Partly as a consequence of these steps, U.S. beef exports exceeded 2003 levels for the first time in 2011, reaching $5.4 billion. Similarly, 57 countries, including many important emerging markets, have now lifted bans on U.S. poultry products. Between 2007 and 2011, the value of U.S. poultry exports increased from $4.1 billion to $5.6 billion. U.S. pork exports to the rapidly growing Chinese market soared, once H1N1-related bans were lifted. Immediately prior to the ban, the U.S. exported on average about $11 million in pork and pork products per month to China. In 2010, pork exports to China totaled only $79.3 million. In 2011, pork exports to China grew by a factor of six, exceeding $477 million and quickly demonstrating the value of better access to this key emerging market. In the first quarter of 2012, roughly two years after the ban was lifted, the U.S. exported about $122 million in pork and pork products to China.

The Obama Administration is also pursuing a broader regional free trade agreement—the Trans-Pacific Partnership (TPP) to further expand export opportunities for American farmers, ranchers and food processors. Current negotiating parties include Australia, Brunei Darussalam, Chile, Malaysia, New Zealand, Peru, Singapore, and Vietnam. Canada, Japan, Mexico, and other countries have signaled interest in joining. Through this agreement, the Administration is seeking to boost U.S. economic growth and support the creation and retention of high-quality jobs at home by increasing American exports to a region that includes some of the world's most dynamic emerging economies and represents more than 40 percent of global trade.

In addition, Russia's accession to the World Trade Organization (WTO) is a top priority for the Obama Administration. The Administration worked closely with Russia to secure commitments that will enhance the transparency and predictability of Russia's trade regime once it joins the WTO, thus creating more certainty and opportunities for U.S. agricultural exporters. For our farmers and ranchers to benefit from Russia's WTO commitments, Congress will need to terminate the application of Jackson Vanik amendment so that the President can grant Russia Permanent Normal Trade Relations (PNTR).

Box 2: Focus on Emerging Markets under the National Export Initiative

Growing demand from emerging markets has played an important role in driving the U.S. agricultural export recovery. During 2000-10, world population rose on average 77 million people per year. This population growth was concentrated in developing countries, where per capita incomes have also been rising. As countries move from low-income to middle-income status and as populations in these countries move from the countryside into cities, diets tend to diversify toward meats and dairy products (and other high-value products such as processed foods). As demand for high value products rises, imports tend to rise. U.S. agriculture benefits from this growth in two ways. As demand shifts from staples to high-value products, the demand for grains and oilseeds as feed often rises to support growing livestock sectors. The United States is very competitive in grains and oilseeds as well as other high-value agricultural products, and stands to benefit as emerging markets become steadily more important consumers of U.S. agricultural exports. These shifts, and the benefits they are bringing to American agriculture, are already highly visible in some commodity markets. China, for example, is now the largest importer of U.S. soybeans, consuming more than half of all U.S. soybean exports.

For the foreseeable future, the growth of demand from developing countries for the output of America's farms and ranches appears to rest on the strong economic foundation, rooted in the rapidly growing private sectors of key emerging markets. China and India, especially, have the potential to grow rapidly for decades. As these giant economies grow wealthier, their demand for agricultural products will continue to increase. Of course, many other smaller emerging markets are also growing at a robust pace. For many, their growth prospects rest on similarly secure foundations.

Thus, although prices for major crops are projected to decline in the near term as global production responds to recent high prices, long-term growth in global demand for agricultural products, in combination with the continued presence of U.S. ethanol demand for corn and EU biodiesel demand for vegetable oils, is likely to keep prices for corn, oilseeds, and other crops historically high. Similarly, the value of U.S. agricultural exports is expected to rise steadily over the next decade (see Figure 7). So long as U.S. exporters can obtain adequate access to these growing markets, strong foreign demand could support continued growth and prosperity in the American farm economy for years to come.

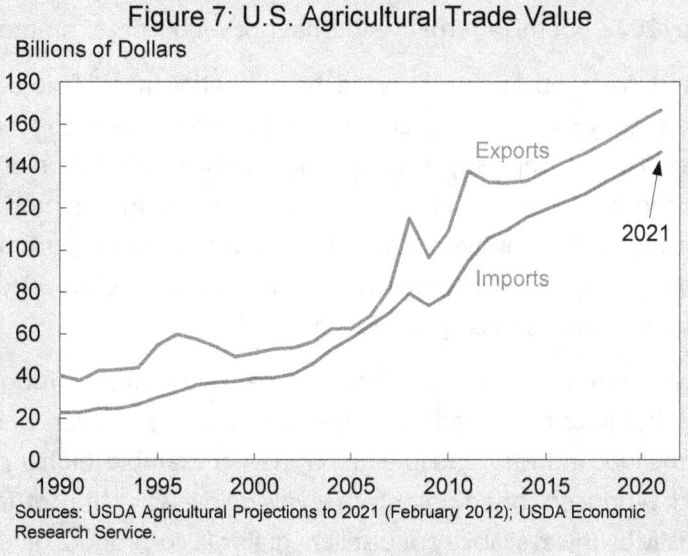

Figure 7: U.S. Agricultural Trade Value

Sources: USDA Agricultural Projections to 2021 (February 2012); USDA Economic Research Service.

The President will continue to work with trading partners around the world to increase market access for our productive farmers and ranchers. The potential benefits of further effort are high. Research by World Bank-affiliated agricultural trade economists shows that the complete elimination of agricultural trade barriers could raise the level of U.S. exports by nearly $20 billion per year above and beyond what we would expect in the absence of such liberalization (Anderson and Martin, 2006). This kind of far-reaching liberalization would add $168 billion per year to the welfare of global consumers and producers (Anderson 2010).

New Markets at Home as well as Abroad

The agricultural sector has been challenged to provide not just food, feed, and fiber to U.S. and world consumers, but also to meet a larger share of our nation's transportation fuel needs. Farmers, ranchers, and forest managers have responded and the production of renewable and clean bioenergy dramatically increased over the past five years, contributing to an all-of-the-above energy strategy. In addition, as farms have restructured and re-organized to take advantage of technical progress they have specialized as well. More farms are producing organic and specialty products and income earned from agritourism and biobased products is increasing.

Energy for today's transportation

Currently, the predominant biofuel in the United States is corn-based ethanol and, to a lesser extent, biomass-based biodiesel. In 2012, the United States is on pace to produce more than 14 billion gallons of corn ethanol, accounting for nearly 40% of total U.S. corn use. Increasing the volumes of gasoline substitutes helps drive down prices when biofuel feedstocks are cheap relative to crude oil. Researchers have linked the increasing supply of ethanol between 2000 and 2010 to a drop in gasoline prices of approximately $0.29 per gallon on average (see Du and Hayes, 2011). In addition, the U.S. produced 967 million gallons of biodiesel in 2011—drawn from soybean oil (about 20% of current use) and other feedstocks. Cellulosic ethanol made from non-food feedstocks such as corn stover, grasses, or forestry products are scheduled to become a much more substantial share (16 out of 36 billion gallons) of our renewable fuel supply by 2022, but this alternative fuel has not yet become commercially widespread.

Rising gasoline and diesel prices globally have boosted the competitiveness of biofuel production in the United States and subsequently created a new and growing source of demand for conventional commodity feedstocks (particularly corn and soybean oil in the U.S.). Since 2007, corn prices have generally risen in tandem with ethanol production, resulting in higher incomes from corn production, and causing adjustments in the allocation of land between crops. Initially, the growth of corn production came at the expense of soybeans, cotton, and other crops that compete with corn, but price signals have since induced farmers to bring more land into crop production.

Higher commodity prices, caused by a variety of factors, have contributed to rising farm incomes and U.S. agricultural exports, but have presented challenges for downstream users of commodities, such as livestock producers, the food industry, and foreign buyers. For example, higher prices for corn have raised costs for livestock producers, bringing output levels below what they otherwise would have been. This is offset partially by the availability of distillers' grains (a co-product of ethanol production) as a substitute source for feed. The shift to "next generation" biofuels—those produced from non-food feedstocks and wastes—will change the resources used for biofuel production, when they become commercially viable. The use of feedstocks that do not compete directly with conventional commodity crops will have a smaller effect on land use as well as food and feed markets.

Raising agricultural productivity growth and diversifying the source of feedstocks for bioenergy production will mitigate many of the concerns associated with corn-based ethanol and soy-based biodiesel production. In addition, as yields increase for conventional feedstocks such as corn and soybeans the price impacts of biofuel demand will fall, lowering prices for food and livestock feed. Further, the shift to "next generation" biofuels and bioenergy produced from non-food feedstocks and wastes, such as biodiesel from algae and bioelectricity from manure, will change the resources used for bioenergy production. Feedstocks could increasingly come from crop residues, energy crops such as switchgrass and fast growing woody biomass. The use of these feedstocks will have a smaller direct impact on food and feed markets.

Investing in Tomorrow's Renewable Energy

The Administration is supporting advances in bioenergy through such programs as the Biomass Crop Assistance Program, the Biorefinery Assistance Program, the Repowering Assistance Program and the Bioenergy Program for Advanced Biofuels, and Rural Energy for America Program. Implementation of the 2008 Farm Bill has contributed to USDA's efforts to revitalize the rural economy and meet the Nation's energy challenges. Those renewable energy programs provided new sources of farm income, increased domestic energy production and developed a domestic renewable energy industry which helped create jobs and reduce America's dependence on imported oil. For example, since 2003, through the Rural Energy for America Program (REAP), the USDA has invested more than $350 million in grants and loans in more than 5000 renewable energy and energy efficiency projects that have helped generate or save 6.5 million megawatts hours of power, enough to fuel 600,000 households.

The Recovery Act made substantial investments in America's renewable energy future. In the short term, those investments have helped keep the U.S. on track to achieve the President's goal of doubling renewable energy production by 2012. Over the long term, those investments will help ensure that renewable energy sources become a major part of our energy supply. Increasing geothermal, wind, solar, and biomass renewable energy production will increase incomes, particularly for residents of rural communities.

States with largely rural populations have some of the highest technical potential for renewable development and therefore will likely be the principal recipients of renewable energy projects spurred by these Federal incentives. Installed wind capacity has increased from about 25,000 MW at the end of 2008 to almost 47,000 MW by the end of 2011. States with installed capacity greater than 1,000 MW include Colorado, Indiana, Kansas New York, Wyoming, North Dakota, Oklahoma, Oregon, Washington, Minnesota, Illinois, California, Iowa, and Texas. Since 2009, capacity has increased by 35%. In just the past three years, capacity in Ohio, Arizona, Nebraska, Maine, South Dakota, Michigan, Massachusetts, Idaho, and Vermont has increased by more than 100%.[4] Low-density rural counties have the greatest

---

4. See www.windpoweringamerica.gov/wind_installed_capacity.asp.

technical potential for solar and wind-based energy, while high-density rural counties have the greatest technical potential for crop and forestry biomass as well as renewable energy from animal waste residues. In particular, North Dakota, Montana, and other Great Plains states rank highest in terms of wind intensity (see Figure 8).

The Administration has also provided support to increasing the availability of renewable fuels (see the recently released *National Bioeconomy Blueprint* for more details). For example, in September 2011, USDA's Agricultural and Food Research Initiative committed more than $136 million to develop regional Coordinated Agricultural Projects for bioenergy systems through partnerships between academia, government, and industry. Plants Engineered to Replace Oil (PETRO) is a $30 million program launched recently by the Advanced Research Projects Agency-Energy (ARPA-E) aims to create plants that capture more energy from sunlight and convert that energy directly into fuels by optimizing processes of energy capture and conversion to develop robust, farm-ready crops that deliver more energy per acre with less processing prior to delivery to retailers. In August, 2011, under the USDA-DOE Plant Feedstock Genomics for Bioenergy Program, $12.2 million was awarded for research to improve special crops for biofuels by increasing their yield, quality, and ability to adapt to extreme environments. Relying on modern genomics to develop novel breeding strategies, researchers focused on switchgrass, poplar trees, sorghum, miscanthus, and energy cane, among other promising plants with potential for growth, on marginal lands that are poorly suited for food crops. Potential benefits of this research range from decreasing oil consumption to increasing options for American farmers, while adding new jobs and driving wealth creation in rural America.

Domestic production of renewable energy, including bioenergy, is a national imperative. Reducing dependence on foreign energy by expanding domestic renewable fuels has impacts on the overall U.S. economy because of energy's importance in consumption, production, and trade. As production technology advances and petroleum prices continue to rise as projected, the benefits to renewable bioenergy will also increase. By substituting domestic biofuels for imported petroleum, for example, the United States would pay less for imports overall and receive higher prices for exports, providing a gain for the economy from favorable terms of trade. U.S. household consumption would rise because of higher real wages, increased household income, and lower import prices (ERS, 2010 ERR-102). As noted above, USDA has been working to assist in developing competitive bioenergy sources, which will increase production opportunities for farmers, help create jobs, combat global warming, replace our dependence on foreign oil and strengthen a 21st century economy that is built to last.

Box 3: More than a quarter million organic cows.

Organic farming has been one of the fastest growing sectors in agriculture. Between 2002 and 2008, acres under organic production grew on average by 16.5 percent annually. In 1997, the retail value of organic food sales totaled $3.6 billion; in 2008 they totaled $21.1 billion. That growth has been particularly evident in the organic dairy sector, accounting for 16 percent of organic sales in 2008. The number of organic milk cows on US farms increased by annual average of 26 percent between 2000 and 2008 (see Figure 9), for example (USDA, ERS, ERR-82). The CROPP cooperative, for example, was founded in Wisconsin by seven small farm families in 1988. Now it is one of the largest organic cooperatives in the U.S. representing 1,687 farmers. The cooperative sold more than $715 million in organic products under its *Organic Valley* and *Organic Prairie* labels in 2011 up from $523 million in 2009 (about 85% of sales are liquid milk). The coop-erative lists several benefits to being a member: stabilizing prices, providing brand recognition, technical assistance, certification, and marketing power. Profits for the cooperative exceeded $13 million in 2011, up from $7 million in 2009.

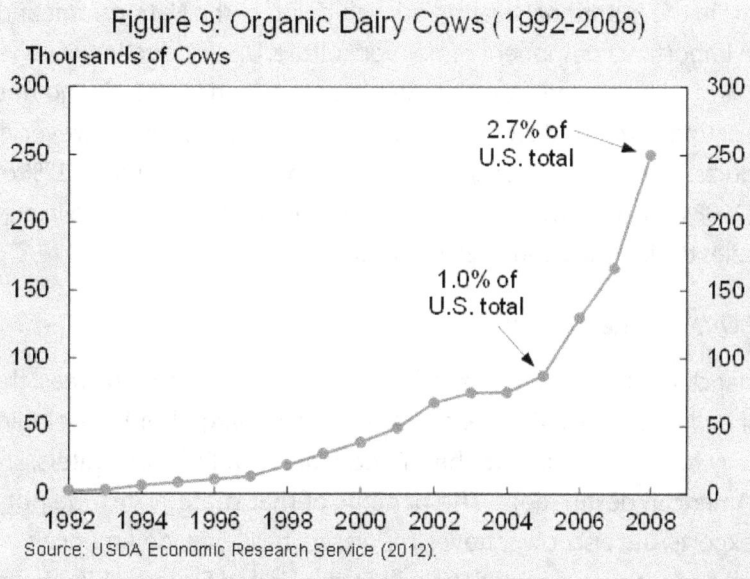

Figure 9: Organic Dairy Cows (1992-2008)

Source: USDA Economic Research Service (2012).

Organic Crops

Investments in research and development and progress made to minimize trade barriers also benefits specialty markets, such as in organic agriculture. In 2009, for example, the U.S. signed an organic equiva-lence arrangement with Canada which allows organic products certified in one country to be sold as such in the other. This is particularly important for small and mid-sized operations that cannot afford the time and money necessary for duplicative certifications, fees, and inspections. In February, 2012, the U.S. established a similar equivalence arrangement with the European Union (EU). To ensure that the terms of all trade agreements are being met, the National Organic Program conducts periodic audits of foreign countries' organic programs. Between 2009 and 2011, USDA has supported internal science and university researchers with more than $117 million focused on improving the productivity and success of organic agriculture. For example, USDA research on weed management research for organic vegetable production has produced techniques and tools that can help control 70% of weeds at 15% of the cost of hiring workers to weed by hand. Extending USDA organic research findings to people in the field is critical and the "eOrganic" electronic extension service funded by USDA has become an essential tool for compiling and disseminating knowledge about organic production. The retail value of the organic industry grew to $31.4 billion, up from $21.1 billion in 2008 and from $3.6 billion in 1997 (Dimitri and Oberholtzer 2009; USDA 2011). Organic foods continue to gain market share in the food industry, climbing to 4.2% of U.S. retail food sales in 2010. This creates opportunities for farmers and ranchers: the number of operations certified organic grew by 1,109—or more than 6%—between 2009 and 2011.

Other Specialty Crops

U.S. producers have also turned to horticulture to take advantage of niche local markets as well as new export opportunities. Horticultural crop production is a diverse, complex, management-intensive, and little-subsidized business in the United States. It is also among the more financially successful components of U.S. agriculture. Along with fruits and nuts, vegetables and melons have long been recognized as vital components in the nutritional health and well-being of the Nation. Fruit and vegetable[5] farms, for example, are an important component of U.S. agriculture. U.S. production of vegetables and melons occurs on about 2% of all harvested cropland. Similarly, production of fruit and tree nuts is harvested from less than 2% of total harvested cropland. From that small footprint, however, comes a diverse set of high-value products. Vegetable, melons, and tree fruits and nuts generated 22% of all farm crop cash receipts between 2008 and 2010. That produce accounts for about $16 billion in export sales annually, or 16% of export sales during the 2008 to 2011 period.[6]

Agritourism and Outdoor Recreation

Committed to enhancing job growth and economic development in rural areas, the President signed an Executive Order on January 19, 2012, creating a Task Force charged with developing a National Travel and Tourism Strategy to promote visits to the United States public lands, waters, shores, monuments, and other iconic American destinations. The benefits of that strategy include not only the potential increase in travel exports, but also lower travel imports as it will provide Americans with more and better choices of travel and tourism destinations within the United States. While the government has an important role in insuring that national treasures such as Yellowstone National Park are appropriately maintained and made accessible to domestic and international tourists, rural areas also provide many recreational opportunities.

In 2006, for example, the Outdoor Industry Foundation, estimated that active outdoor recreation participants spent nearly $300 billion on recreational trips and outdoor gear in 2006.[7] These figures include outdoor activities such as fishing, hunting, hiking, biking, camping, paddling, wildlife viewing, and snow sports. Hunting and fishing and other outdoor recreational pursuits also provide an additional source

---

5. Vegetables include all fresh and processed vegetables (potatoes, sweet potatoes, dry beans, dry peas, and lentils).

6. usda.mannlib.cornell.edu/MannUsda/viewDocumentInfo.do?documentID=1377; www.ers.usda.gov/Publications/vgs/#yearbook; www.ers.usda.gov/Publications/fts/#yearbook; www.ers.usda.gov/Data/FarmIncome/finfidmu.htm

7. Southwick Associates and the Outdoor Industry Foundation. 2006. *The Active Outdoor Recreation Economy: A $730 Billion Annual Contribution to the U.S. Economy.* http://www.outdoorindustry.org/images/researchfiles/RecEconomypublic.pdf?26

of income to farmers, ranchers, and forest landowners. In 2006, 34 million hunters and anglers alone spent over $76 billion, including trip-related expenses ($24.6 billion), equipment costs ($41.0 billion) and other expenditures ($11.1 billion) for items like magazines, permits, concession fees, etc.[8] The President recognizes the important economic benefits of outdoor recreation to rural economies and has directed his cabinet to develop the America's Great Outdoors Initiative. The America's Great Outdoors Initiative aims to reconnect Americans to the great outdoors, invest in a shared conservation legacy, and sustain job creation in vibrant rural economies.

Rural areas also provide recreational opportunities on farms, known as agritourism. Farm-based recreation includes outdoor recreation, such as hunting, fishing, and horseback riding. However, agritourism also includes entertainment activities, such as hayrides, petting zoos, corn mazes, wine tours, and wildlife viewing, plus hospitality services such as on-farm bed and breakfasts, weddings, and other events. Agritourism generated $567 million in gross cash farm income in 2007, mostly on small to intermediate farms (total farm sales less than $250,000, operator reports farming as principal occupation), double the amount recorded in 2002. Data indicates that agritourism in the U.S. is particularly concentrated in the Southern Plains. The more detailed 2007 Census of Agriculture data show that regional concentrations also occur in parts of the West, Southeast, and in some high-amenity locations such as in New England, the East coast, and along the Northern Great Lakes (Bagi and Reeder, 2011).

Figure 10: Locations of Biobased Firms

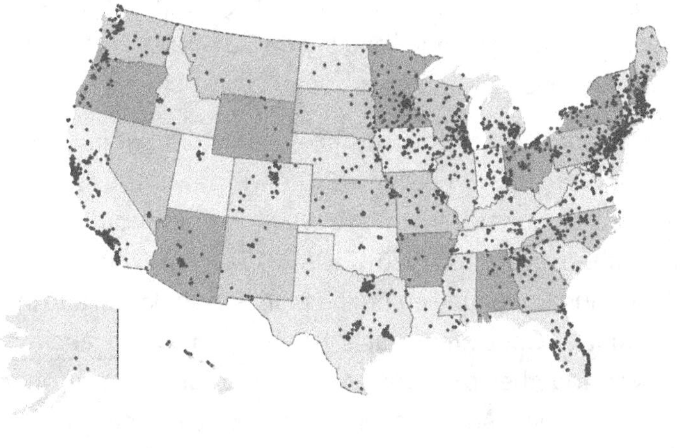

Source: USDA BioPreferred Program.

Biobased Economy

More than 3,000 companies in the United States are producing biobased products (see Figure 10). Paper and Textile industries have moved toward biobased products and away from use of petrochemical products for both manufacturing and clean-up, and now use microorganisms or biologically derived industrial enzymes that are more environmentally friendly and cost effective. In the future, biological innovation could lead to developments, such as improved biological systems for removing carbon dioxide directly from air and sequestering it in biomass for other uses. From traditional plant breeding to synthetic biology, medical treatments to petroleum replacements, future bio-manufacturing will be greatly facilitated by the ability to design and use biological systems and organisms quickly. Such opportunities offer agricultural producers expanded markets for their products.

---

8. U.S. Department of the Interior, Fish and Wildlife Service, and U.S. Department of Commerce, U.S. Census Bureau. 2006 National Survey of Fishing, Hunting, and Wildlife-Associated Recreation.

The recently augmented BioPreferred Program at USDA highlights new opportunities to supplement farm production, support economic expansion and create jobs from the farm to the finished product.[9]

Toward a Greater Harvest: the Future of American Agriculture

The U.S. agricultural economy has quickly bounced back from the worst global downturn since the Great Depression. That resilience was forged through nearly three decades of difficult adjustment after the farm crisis of the early 1980s. Building off sustained public and private investments in R&D, productivity growth, and market diversification, farms and ranches restructured and became more efficient. Farmers quickly adopted new and promising technologies, developed through public research and development. They also specialized in management operations—contracting out for capital-intensive services that require expensive machinery and for information services and organizing more effective contracting arrangement to limit exposure to risk. Farmers reliance on borrowing went down. In 2007, 31% of farms used debt financing, compared to 60% in 1986 (Henderson and Akers, 2010). Current levels of debt are now well below debt repayment capacity. The Federal government restructured farm supports so as to minimize distorting planting decisions and supported eliminating trade barriers, while improving the safety net for risk mitigation. The strength of the farm lenders (rural commercial banks and the Farm Credit System) also benefits the agricultural economy and helps ensure favorable access to credit to farmers (Sundell and Shane, 2012). Markets opened, yields improved, and the agricultural economy recovered—but it took time.

America's agriculture economy faces an historic set of opportunities. Farm sector income reached a nominal record of $98.1 billion in 2011, which was the 4th highest real farm income in the last 50 years. Real equity of farms is expected to establish a new nominal record in 2012, with the value of farm assets at the highest level since 1980 (USDA 2012). Farm exports are at record levels, as is America's agricultural trade surplus. Continued emerging market population and income growth presents sustained growth opportunities. Government (at all levels), farmers and ranchers, agribusinesses, and local communities must work together to ensure that America's agricultural economy makes the most of this historic opportunity. The Obama Administration has set out a strategy for growth in this vital sector that emphasizes the following themes.

Investing in Agricultural Research

Even relatively large farms and ranches in the United States constitute a very small share of total agricultural production. This creates a challenge for any farmer or rancher who would want to invest in new crops or new techniques—others would quickly copy these improvements, limiting the profits accruing to the innovator. In recognition of the special challenges faced by would-be innovators in agriculture, the U.S. has always pioneered agricultural research efforts, leading the world through the 19th century and into the 20th century. The benefits from past R&D investments helped producers become more efficient following the 1980's crisis in the agricultural economy However, in recent years, the U.S. has cut back on many kinds of agricultural research. As a result, increases in agricultural productivity appear to

---

9. See program website for additional details: www.biopreferred.gov

be tapering, suggesting that revived investment in agricultural R&D will be needed to maintain America's competitive advantage in producing from the land those products that generate the highest net returns.

The potential returns to increased research investment are particularly high today. New markets are opening abroad for new products; scientists are increasingly noting adverse changes to climatic conditions for growing crops and raising livestock; and other countries are increasing their own exports of traditional and non-traditional commodities. In addition, meeting the food needs of an expected 2050 global population of 9 billion will require agricultural production to increase by 70%; demands for bioenergy supplies are increasing as petroleum prices rise; and consumers' preferences for cleaner air and water are increasing.

These challenges will require supportive investment policies for basic and applied agricultural research, to ensure that U.S. agricultural productivity continues to increase. The Administration plans to capitalize on those diverse opportunities and invest in future innovations, such as more productive crops, healthier livestock, and adaptive farming practices for weather extremes by requesting $2.3 billion our 2013 Budget for agricultural research and development (R&D).

Doubling Exports Can Start with Agriculture

Thanks to food and agricultural exports, the United States is well on the way to doubling exports as envisioned by President Obama. To realize the promise of continued growth, the Administration is negotiating for greater access to sell American agricultural products in important Asian markets through the TPP, exploring greater economic opportunities with the European Union and eliminating unwarranted barriers to American grown products around the world. Central to the Administration's international trade policy, the United States is focused on lowering trade barriers around the world to increase opportunities for U.S. farmers and ranchers, capitalizing on America's large endowment of arable land and its high level of agricultural technology.

Opportunities at Home

Rising prices for fossil fuels have increased the opportunity for U.S. agriculture to participate in markets for biofuels, wind power, biomass and biogas electricity generation. Maintaining policies that promote domestic energy alternatives provides increasing opportunities for U.S. agriculture to contribute to U.S. energy security and greenhouse gas mitigation goals.

Similarly, domestic investments in small business will be essential to developing the kinds of innovative rural business and manufacturing needed to spur jobs. For example, in August the White House Rural Council established a rural "carve-out" in the Small Business Investment Company (SBIC) Impact Investment Program that will invest in distressed areas and emerging sectors such as clean energy. SBA will provide up to a 2:1 match to private capital raised by the fund. SBA and USDA are committed to partnering to drive $350 million of investment capital through the fund and existing SBICs into rural small businesses over five years, doubling the current rate of investment.

Those efforts are geared toward helping rural businesses become more competitive and expanding opportunities for agricultural production at home and abroad in markets for bioenergy and for other non-traditional farm products, such as organics and other high-valued crops. The diversification of the growing agricultural economy spans new products for exports, to agritourism and outdoor recreation opportunities, to new biobased product manufacturing.

America's Agricultural Revival: Today, Tomorrow, and Beyond

America began as an agricultural economy, and our first President dreamed that we would someday become, in his prescient words, "a granary and a storehouse for the world." Throughout our history, the innovation of America's farmers and ranchers has lit a pathway to progress for the world, creating new products and processes that fed our own nation as well as millions beyond our shores. As a new century of progress and achievement in American agriculture unfolds, America's farmers and ranchers continue to define the frontiers of agricultural best practice. In recent years, it has become increasingly clear that American agriculture has put two decades of difficult transition behind it.

- American agriculture has never been stronger, more innovative, or more competitive than it is today.

- The productivity of our farm and ranches remains among the very highest in the world.

- Food and agricultural products are one of the country's most important exports.

As this report has demonstrated, America's agricultural economy and its rural communities face an unparalleled opportunity for growth and prosperity. This is not just an historic moment of opportunity for rural communities—it is one for the nation as a whole.

This report has laid out a strategy for smart, cost-effective government action that could keep America's agriculture economy in high gear for decades to come. If fully implemented, this pro-growth agenda could support the broader national goals of increasing domestic energy security and expanding exports. Our hope is that this report will not only highlight the Administration's achievements and the potential of America's agricultural economy, but help build the consensus needed to establish and maintain the smart public policies that will enable this enormous potential to be realized. Our nation's farmers and ranchers, and the future generations who will inherit their land, their dreams, and their legacy, deserve no less.

Citations

Ali, Mir, and Gary Lucier. 2011. "Financial Characteristics of Vegetable and Melon Farms." *Outlook Report VGS-342-01*. USDA-Economic Research Service. February.

Alston J.M., M.A. Andersen, J.S. James, and P.G. Pardey. 2010. *Persistence Pays: U.S. Agricultural Productivity Growth and the Benefits of Public R&D Spending*. New York: Springer Press.

Alston, Julian M., Michele C. Marra, Philip G. Pardey, and T.J. Wyatt. 2010. "Research Returns Redux: a Meta-Analysis of the Returns to Agricultural R&D." *Australian Journal of Agricultural and Resource Economics*. 44(2): 185-215.

Anderson. Kym. 2010. "Krueger, Schiff, and Valdés Revisited: Agricultural Price and Trade Policy Reform in Developing Countries since 1960." *Applied Economic Perspectives and Policy* 32, no. 2: 195–231.

Bagi, Faqir, and R. Reeder. 2011. "Location of Agritourism Farms Affected by Amenities." *Amber Waves* 9 (1): 40.

Baker, A., and S. Zahniser. 2007. "Ethanol Reshapes the Corn Market." *Amber Waves*. USDA-Economic Research Service. May.

Biomass Research and Development Board. 2008. "Increasing Feedstock Production for Biofuels, Economic Drivers, Environmental Implications, and the Role of Research." U.S. Department of Agriculture. December.

Claassen R., V. Breneman, S. Bucholtz, A. Cattaneo, R. Johansson, and M. Morehart. 2004. "Environmental Compliance in Agricultural Policy: Past Performance and Future Potential." AER-832, USDA-Economic Research Service. June.

Coyle, W. 2010. "Next-Generation Biofuels: Near-Term Challenges and Implications for Agriculture," *Outlook Report BIO-01-01*. USDA-Economic Research Service. May.

Dimitri, Carolyn, and Lydia Oberholtzer. 2009. "Marketing U.S. Organic Foods: Recent Trends From Farms to Consumers." *Economic Information Bulletin*, no.58: 33. September.

Evenson, Robert E. 2001. "Economic Impacts of Agricultural Research and Extension." In *Handbook of Agricultural Economics*, edited by B.L. Gardner and G. C. Rausser. London: Elsevier.

Fernandez-Cornejo, J. 2011. "Adoption of Genetically Engineered Crops in the U.S." USDA-Economic Research Service. July.

Fernandez-Cornejo, J. and M. Caswell. 2006. "The First Decade of Genetically Engineered Crops in the United States." EIB-11, USDA-Economic Research Service. April.

Fernandez-Cornejo, J. with contributions from A. Mishra, R. Nehring, C. Hendricks, A. Gregory, and M. Southern. 2007. "Off-Farm Income, Technology Adoption and Farm Economic Performance." USDA-Economic Research Service, no.36: 46. February.

Fuglie, Keith, et al. 2011. "Research Investments and Market Structure in the Food Processing, Agricultural Input, and Biofuel Industries Worldwide," USDA-Economic Research Service, no. 130. December.

Fuglie, Keith, James M. MacDonald, and Eldon Ball. 2007. "Productivity Growth in U.S. Agriculture." Economic Brief 9: 5. Economic Research Service. September.

Fuglie, Keith, and P. Heisey. 2007. "Economic Returns to Public Agricultural Research."

Economic Brief no.10. USDA, Economic Research Service. September.

Gehlhar, M., Ashley Winston, and Agapi Somwaru. 2010. "Effects of Increased Biofuels on the U.S. Economy in 2022." *ERR 102*. USDA, Economic Research Service. November.

Heisey, Paul W., John L. King, Kelly Day Rubenstein, Dale A. Bucks, and Rick Welsh. 2010. "Assessing the Benefits of Public Research Within an Economic Framework: The Case of USDA's Agricultural Research Service." *ERR 95*. USDA, Economic Research Service. May.

Henderson, Jason, and Maria Akers. 2010. "Financial Challenges Facing Farm Enterprises." *The Main Street Economist* Issue 1. Federal Reserve Bank of Kansas City.

Henderson, Jason, and Maria Akers. 2012. "Farm Loan Volumes Rise and Agricultural Finances Strengthen." *Agricultural Finance Databook*. Federal Reserve Bank of Kansas City. April.

Jorgenson, Dale W., Mun Ho, and Jon Samuels. 2010. *Information Technology and U.S. Productivity Growth: Evidence from a Prototype Industry Production Account*. The MIT Press. November.

Leibtag, E. 2008. "Corn Prices Hit Record High, But What About Food Costs?" *Amber Waves*. USDA-Economic Research Service. February.

Malcolm, S., M. Aillery, and M. Weinberg. 2009. "Ethanol and a Changing Landscape." *ERR-86*. USDA-Economic Research Service. November.

National Research Council. 2010. *The Impact of Genetically Engineered Crops on Farm Sustainability in the United States*. Washington DC: The National Academies Press. April.

Natural Resource Inventory. National Resource Conservation Service, U.S. Department of Agriculture.

Organization for Economic and Community Development (OECD). 2009. *The role of agriculture and farm household diversification in the rural economy: Evidence and initial policy implications*.

O'Donoghue, Erik J., et al. 2011. "The Changing Organization of U.S. Farming." *Economic Information Bulletin*, no. 83: 65. December.

Rosen, S., and S. Shapouri. 2008. "Rising Food Prices Intensify Food Insecurity in Developing Countries." *Amber Waves*. USDA-Economic Research Service. February.

Sundell, Paul and Mathew Shane. 2012. "The 2008-09 Recession and Recovery: Implications for the Growth and Financial Health of U.S. Agriculture." *Outlook Report WRS-1201*. USDA-Economic Research Service. May.

Trostle, Ronald., et al. 2011. "Why Have Food Commodity Prices Risen Again?" *Outlook Report WRS-1103*. USDA-Economic Research Service. June.

U.S. Department of Agriculture. *2007 Census of Agriculture*, National Agricultural Statistical Service. Washington, DC.

U.S. Department of Agriculture. 2012., "Agricultural Baseline Projections Briefing Room." Economic Research Service. (www.ers.usda.gov/Briefing/Baseline)

U.S. Department of Agriculture. 2010. "Agricultural Trade Multipliers: Effects of Trade on the U.S. Economy." Data Sets, USDA-Economic Research Service. March. (www.ers.usda.gov/Data/TradeMultiplier/econeffects/2010overview.aspx)

U.S. Department of Agriculture. 2012. "Agricultural Trade Multipliers: Effects of Trade on the U.S. Economy." Economic Research Service. March.

U.S. Department of Agriculture. 2012. "Foreign Agricultural Trade of the United States (FATUS)," Data Sets, Economic Research Service. April. (www.ers.usda.gov/Data/Fatus).

U.S. Department of Agriculture. 2012. "Fruit and Tree Nuts Briefing Room." Economic Research Service. (www.ers.usda.gov/Briefing/FruitandTreeNuts).

U.S. Department of Agriculture. 2012. "Fruit and Tree Nuts Yearbook tables." Economic Research Service. (www.ers.usda.gov/publications/FTS/index.htm#yearbook).

U.S. Department of Agriculture. 2012. "Statistics: Farm, Rural, and Natural Resources Indicators," *Amber Waves*, Economic Research Service. March. (www.ers.usda.gov/AmberWaves/March12/Indicators/Indicators.htm).

U.S. Department of Agriculture. 2012. "The Impact of the Rural Energy for America Program on Promoting Energy Efficiency and Renewable Energy." *Rural Development Report*. March.

U.S. Department of Agriculture. 2012. "U.S. and State Farm Income and Wealth Statistics." Economic Research Service. Farm Income: Data Files. (www.ers.usda.gov/data/FarmIncome/finfidmu.htm).

U.S. Department of Agriculture. 2012. "USDA Accomplishments 2009 – 2011: Organic Agriculture."

U.S. Department of Agriculture. 2012. "Vegetables and Melons Briefing Room." Economic Research Service. (www.ers.usda.gov/Briefing/Vegetables/).

U.S. Department of Agriculture. 2012. "Vegetables and Melons Yearbook Tables." Economic Research Service. (www.ers.usda.gov/publications/vgs/#yearbook).

Wainio, John, Mark Gehlhar, and John Dyck. 2011. "Selected Trade Agreements and Implications for U.S. Agriculture." ERR-115. USDA-Economic Research Service. April.

Wallender, S., R. Claasen, and C. Nickerson. 2011. "The Ethanol Decade: An Expansion of U.S. Corn Production, 2000-09." USDA-Economic Research Service. August.

Westcott, P. 2007. "U.S. Ethanol Expansion Driving Changes Throughout the Agricultural Sector." *Amber Waves*. USDA-Economic Research Service. September.

Westcott, P. 2007. "Ethanol Expansion in the United States, How Will the Agricultural Sector Adjust?" *Outlook Report FDS-07D-01*. USDA-Economic Research Service. May.

Wiebe, Keith, and Noel Gollehon. 2006. "Agricultural Resources and Environmental Indicators." ERR 16, USDA-Economic Research Service. July.

www.ingramcontent.com/pod-product-compliance
Lightning Source LLC
Chambersburg PA
CBHW081248170526
45165CB00009B/3239